Original title:
Romance Dance

Editor: Jessica Elisabeth Luik
Author: Daisy Dewi
ISBN HARDBACK: 978-9916-86-066-3
ISBN PAPERBACK: 978-9916-86-067-0

Seaside Sway

The waves dance to the moon's soft gleam
As stars in night do brightly beam
Sand beneath my feet, cool and kind
A soothing balm for weary mind

Seagulls cry as breezes play
In tune with ocean's gentle sway
Footprints traced along the shore
Memories caught forevermore

Shells they whisper ancient tales
Of pirates' gold and mermaids' sails
Night's serenity holds me close
In this seaside drift, I repose

Sunset Serenade

Hues of orange, pink, and gold
Across the sky, a story told
The sun dips low, day's curtain falls
A symphony in twilight's halls

Whispers of the evening breeze
Through leaves that dance above the trees
Nature's song in twilight played
A perfect sunset serenade

Birds retreat to nests of rest
As sky transforms in vast behest
Moments caught between the day
And starlit night’s grand ballet

Tendering Twirl

A twirl beneath the evening sky
With whispered dreams that never die
Hearts embraced in gentle spin
The dance of love does now begin

Eyes that speak without a sound
In this tender space they've found
Every move a silent word
In this dance, love's song is heard

In the moon's soft silver glow
Hearts align, as pure as snow
The world fades in a tender blur
In love's sweet and endless twirl

Whirlwind of Hearts

In the depths of fervent eyes
A storm of passion deeply lies
Hearts like leaves in autumn's grip
In whirlwinds of emotion flip

Kisses stolen, breaths collide
In this tempest, none can hide
Moments swift yet deeply felt
Where love's fierce energy is dealt

In the chaos, calm persists
A harmony that can't resist
Bound by winds of ardent fire
Whirlwind hearts in sweet desire

Rhythm of Affection

In the softness of a whisper
Love's cadence softly beats
Two souls move to the music
In a dance, so sweet, so neat

Hand to hand, heart to heart
In harmony, they sway
Each step, a pledge of unity
In love's rhythm, they stay

Eyes meeting, timeless grace
A waltz of tender care
Every twirl, a promise
In love's affectionate snare

Through the dusk and dawn
They glide without a sound
Bound by the rhythm of affection
Where true love is found

Moments blend together
In a tune of pure devotion
Love's song, their guiding light
Amid the waves of emotion

Paso Doble of Passion

In the fervor of the night
Two figures take the stage
With every fiery glance
Their passions they engage

Footsteps sharp, deliberate
In passion's bold embrace
The dance floor turns to fire
As heartbeats set the pace

Intensity, electric air
Each move a flaming spark
A symphony of desire
Igniting through the dark

Their bodies weave a story
Of love's relentless chase
A paso doble's fervor
In every heated trace

When the final note is played
And shadows draw their part
The echoes of their passion
Remain within the heart

Embrace of the Ballroom

Silken gowns and sapphire eyes
Grace the ballroom's gleam
Where stars align in evening's light
And lovers dare to dream

Each step, a silent whisper
In the grand nocturnal hall
Beneath the crystal chandelier
Where hearts, united, fall

To the melody of romance
They glide in perfect time
In the embrace of the ballroom
Their spirits are sublime

Whispers soft as moonlight
Glances warm as fire
In the waltz of endless moments
They lift their love, entire

As the music slowly fades
And dawn begins to break
The ballroom's gentle embrace
Their love, it leaves awake

Whirlwind of Hearts

Beneath a sky of endless stars
Two lovers find their start
In a whirlwind of unity
Dancing, heart to heart

Their steps are set in motion
By music wild and free
Swirling through the twilight
In sync with destiny

The world becomes a blur
As passion takes the lead
In the whirlwind of hearts
Fulfilled by love's own creed

Every twirl and every spin
A testament to grace
In an endless, joyous whirlwind
Together they embrace

When the night surrenders
To the dawn's first light
The whirlwind of their hearts
Will guide them through the night

Tender Groove

In twilight's embrace, soft melodies play,
Hearts align in the tender groove's sway.
Love serenades with a gentle reprieve,
In the rhythm where souls truly believe.

Soft murmurs ride on the evening's grace,
Steps intertwine in a heavenly place.
As time slows down, a dance to the tune,
Beneath the shy light of an early moon.

Echoes of bliss in the simplest sway,
Moments unfold at the close of the day.
In whispered notes and tender touch shared,
Lives once alone are now beautifully paired.

Whispered Salsas

The night hums softly with secrets unknown,
Feet trace the steps where passion has flown.
Flames of desire in a whispered salsa,
Beneath starry eyes, love's subtle pulse.

Guitars strum patterns of heated beats,
Bodies entwine in rhythm's sweet heat.
Sweat glistens like the dew on dawn's crest,
Hearts syncopate in a sultry rest.

Each step leads deeper into the night,
Eyes locking in an unspoken delight.
Voices silent, but the soul's loud chants,
Sway in the dance that pure love grants.

Waves of Rhythm

Oceans sway with a musical finesse,
Waves crash in time, a natural caress.
The shores receive in rhythmic embrace,
The dance of eternity, an ageless grace.

Seagulls call out in harmonious tune,
Winds whirl around in a lively monsoon.
Nature’s ballet, in pulses, it breathes,
Life in every tide that rises and seethes.

Sand between toes keeps time in the flow,
Heartbeats align with the ocean below.
In the waves of rhythm, we find our place,
Lost in the tempo, in Nature’s own pace.

Swept in Love

Winds whisper tales of hearts' embrace,
Gently nudged by love's tender grace.
Kisses like petals in the breeze,
Swept in love, with utmost ease.

Eyes that glisten, soft and bright,
Love's lanterns in the deepest night.
Warmth that radiates from the core,
Two hearts yearning, forevermore.

In each touch, a promise kept,
In love's arms, dreams are swept.
Silence speaks in tender hues,
In boundless love, we fuse.

Midnight Waltz

Beneath the moon with silver light,
We dance away the quiet night.
Stars above, a gentle guide,
Our hearts align, and dreams collide.

In shadows deep, the hours fly,
With whispered truths and softest sigh.
A timeless rhythm, old, yet new,
The midnight waltz with me and you.

Gliding through the twilight's vein,
With every step, we ease our pain.
Lost in melodies so sweet,
Our souls in harmony complete.

Underneath the tranquil sky,
We let the world around us lie.
Held so close, no words to say,
This waltz will never fade away.

Fusion of Hearts

In moments shared, we find our way,
Two paths converge as night meets day.
A fusion born of tender sparks,
Uniting souls and mending marks.

Hand in hand, we bridge the space,
Finding solace in love's embrace.
Harmony in every beat,
Two hearts as one, our journey sweet.

Through trials faced and fears subdued,
We gather strength in love renewed.
A symphony of trust and care,
Creating echoes everywhere.

Bound by faith and dreams we've spun,
Our hearts entwined, forever one.
Guided by a shining light,
Together, we embrace the night.

Golden Step

With every step, a story told,
In golden hues, our love unfolds.
A dance of light within our eyes,
A promise held beneath the skies.

Through seasons change and passing years,
We stride with joy and conquer fears.
Eternal warmth within our bound,
In golden steps, our love is found.

The sands of time may gently flow,
But in our hearts, the flame will glow.
With grace, we move as one in time,
A melody, a sacred rhyme.

And when the dusk of life descends,
We'll journey on, as lovers, friends.
Together through the sunset's gleam,
Our golden steps, an endless dream.

Stylish Connections

In threads of elegance and flair,
We weave a bond beyond compare.
Stylish whispers, hearts entwined,
A tapestry of souls combined.

With every glance and subtle touch,
We speak in ways that mean so much.
Fashioned love in quiet hues,
A stylish dance of silent cues.

Through highs and lows and worlds unseen,
We craft a tale in shades of green.
A canvas broad with colors bold,
Our stylish connections redefined and told.

In moments still, we understand,
The language of a clasping hand.
A journey rich in love's design,
In every thread, our hearts align.

Serenade of Steps

Upon the wooden floor we glide,
With grace, we move, side by side.
In rhythm, our hearts gently align,
A serenade of steps, purely divine.

Each twirl, a whisper, soft and sweet,
In echoing halls, where dreams meet.
Our shadows dance, a fleeting sight,
Lost in the music of the night.

Beneath the chandeliers' golden gleam,
Two souls in tandem, like a dream.
The melody wraps us in a trance,
As we partake in this endless dance.

Holding close, in silent pledge,
Our footsteps trace the ballroom edge.
Every beat, a lover's vow,
In perfect harmony, here and now.

Lovers' Carousel

Round and round, the carousel turns,
With every spin, our passion burns.
Hand in hand, love's sweet embrace,
Forever caught in endless chase.

Horses painted, dreams untold,
Stories of lovers, brave and bold.
As music plays, so soft and light,
We journey through this magic night.

In your eyes, I see the stars,
A universe that's solely ours.
Our spirits lift with every ride,
On this carousel, side by side.

We laugh, we sigh, in rhythmic dance,
Reveling in our sweet romance.
Eternal, this joy we feel,
Our love, a never-ending wheel.

Pulsing Hearts

Our hearts beat in fervent rhythm,
A symphony of life within them.
Pulsing with a love so true,
In every beat, it's me and you.

Eyes locked, we share a glance,
Lost together in this dance.
The world around us fades away,
In your arms, forever I'd stay.

Each heartbeat, a loving thrum,
A silent song only for some.
Our passion, a fierce fire bright,
Guiding us through each night.

Connected by this tender beat,
Two souls as one, pure and sweet.
In unison, we feel it start,
The timeless echo of pulsing hearts.

Ballroom Bliss

Silken gowns and tailored suits,
Amidst the blooms, their colors mute.
Couples dance in perfect bliss,
Sealing their love with every kiss.

The chandelier lights up the hall,
Casting shadows, soft and tall.
Each movement, a tale anew,
In the ballroom, where dreams come true.

In the melody's gentle sway,
Lovers find their perfect way.
Spins and dips, with grace refine,
Lost in moments, purely divine.

Whispers shared in passion's heat,
As their hearts in rhythm meet.
On the floor, their story told,
In dances timeless, love unfolds.

Celestial Sway

Across the velvet midnight sky,
Twinkling gems on high do lie.
In cosmic dance, they gently play,
In their eternal, quiet sway.

Galaxies in spirals fold,
Nebulae in colors bold.
Through the ether, whispers say,
The universe in grand array.

Planets spin in silent grace,
Each in its predestined place.
Among the stars, we find our way,
In the celestial, timeless sway.

Intertwined Souls

Across the echo of our hearts,
A deeper bond now gently starts.
In silent dreams, our spirits blend,
Intertwined until the end.

Through the maze of life's embrace,
We find our rhythm, face to face.
In shadows cast and daylight's glow,
Our souls entwine, and ever grow.

No words are needed, none bespoke,
A silent vow through touch and stroke.
Our essence weaves its own sweet prose,
Two souls as one, forever close.

Starlit Silhouettes

Beneath the night's celestial dome,
We find ourselves far from home.
Our shadows cast in silver gleams,
In starlit silhouettes of dreams.

The moon lays down its tender rays,
Guiding us through twilight haze.
Hand in hand, we softly tread,
In night's embrace, where dreams are fed.

The whispering winds of distant lands,
Speak of tales from ancient sands.
In this canvas of soft regrets,
We're etched as starlit silhouettes.

Lovers' Waltz

Beneath the chandeliers of night,
In lovers' waltz, we take our flight.
Our hearts align in gentle beats,
As whispers fall in rhythmic treats.

The world around us fades away,
In our embrace, we sweetly sway.
Through time and space, we're locked in trance,
Bound together in this dance.

In silence, secrets softly told,
A timeless love, both young and old.
In lovers' waltz, we find our way,
Together, always to stay.

Steps of Devotion

In quiet steps that hearts do take,
We forge a path through dark and light.
With every promise, none to break,
We vow to weather eve and night.

Through stormy winds and summer's heat,
We dance, two souls in rhythm swell.
The cadence of our hearts will meet,
In every story, love will tell.

With grace, we walk, where shadows fade,
A tapestry of trust unfolds.
No fear can strike, no mark be made,
In sacred whispers, truth we hold.

The world may change, yet steadfast stay,
The love that grows with each sunrise.
In tender moments, here we'll lay,
Gazing deep into each other's eyes.

Come rain or shine, our pledge remains,
Unmoved by tides or passing time.
In every joy, in all the pains,
Our hearts will beat in perfect rhyme.

Twilight Waltz

At twilight's touch, the world is still,
A hush that lingers in the air.
We waltz where dreams and wishes fill,
Our spirits free without a care.

The sky a canvas, hues unfurl,
In whispered tones, the night does call.
Two shadows blend in mystic swirl,
As moonlight paints the trees so tall.

In twilight's glow, we gently sway,
The stars our audience, so bright.
With every step, we drift away,
Into the heart of endless night.

The nightingale sings soft and sweet,
A melody of olden times.
In harmony, our souls will meet,
Entwined by love, a dance of chimes.

As night descends, we find our grace,
In every twirl, in each embrace.
The twilight waltz, our sacred space,
Where love and time do interlace.

Swinging Desires

Beneath the moon, where shadows play,
We find our haven in the trees.
On swings that arch both night and day,
Our hearts are carried by the breeze.

As whispers of the wild night sing,
Our souls take flight, untamed and free.
With every push, a sweeter thing,
Our passions soar, as high as we.

In rhythm with the crickets' song,
Our laughter joins in nature's choir.
The swing of dreams, it won't be long,
Till we ignite with pure desire.

The stars align in trails of fire,
Guiding us through the velvet sky.
In swinging arcs of deep desire,
We touch the heavens, you and I.

Here in this moment, uninhibited,
We fly on swings of love's creation.
An endless evening, exquisite,
Swinging desires, our heart's elation.

Rhythm of Amour

In the quiet rush before dawn's light,
A rhythm pulses deep and true.
It binds us close throughout the night,
In every beat, love's essence grew.

With every thump, a silent vow,
To cherish, honor, hold so dear.
The rhythm of amour, here and now,
Dissolves our every doubt and fear.

We move in sync, no step amiss,
To melodies of hearts that dance.
A symphony of purest bliss,
In every touch, in every glance.

United by this steady tide,
Our spirits bound by unseen thread.
No force on earth could e'er divide,
The rhythm of our love widespread.

And as the sun begins to rise,
Our hearts still beat in harmony.
In rhythm of amour, no lies,
Just you and me, eternally.

Harmony in Motion

A breath of wind, the leaves they dance,
A silent song, a wistful trance.
Nature's rhythm, pulsing through,
A whispered note, through skies so blue.

Rivers wander, mountains stand,
Unified, a timeless band.
The world, a stage, in perfect sync,
Each element, an endless link.

Waves that crash, and tides that turn,
Each pattern set, for us to learn.
A cadence found in waves of grain,
In giving sun, and soulful rain.

Ebb and flow, a life’s delight,
Day and night, and dark to light.
Harmony in Motion, pure,
A cosmic beat that will endure.

Life's ballet, both grand and small,
In every rise, in every fall.
Unified by unseen thread,
'Til time itself lies quiet, dead.

Veil of Stars

A blanket dark, with pins of light,
Illumined dreams that pierce the night.
Each star a wish, a silent cry,
Within the boundless, velvet sky.

Galaxies that spin and weave,
In cosmic dance, they never leave.
A shimmer here, a sparkle there,
Unfolds a universe so rare.

Constellations etched in lore,
Guiding souls forevermore.
The veil of stars, a map divine,
To guide our hearts through space and time.

Tempests rage in stellar seas,
Yet peace is found in such as these.
A cosmic lullaby, so sweet,
Where star and dream and lovers meet.

Through night's enchantment, we are drawn,
To yearn for night, and greet the dawn.
In veils of stars, our spirits soar,
And touch the truths that we adore.

Twilight Embrace

The sun dips low, the skies blush red,
A farewell whispered, softly said.
Day surrenders, night takes flight,
In the arms of twilight's might.

Shadows stretch across the land,
An artist's brush, both soft and grand.
Colors play in gentle beams,
Melding day with tinted dreams.

Birds in flight, their journey ends,
A secret language, twilight sends.
Silent call to close of day,
And open night's enchanting play.

In twilight's hue, the world lies still,
A tranquil hush, a gentle thrill.
Stars prepare their grand debut,
Underneath a sky of blue.

Hold close the dusk, the tender grace,
Embrace the night's approaching face.
For in this hour, all is right,
Between the realms of day and night.

Crimson Rapture

A rose in bloom, a fiery crest,
Nature's heart upon its breast.
Petals bold in fervent red,
A love in sunlight, softly spread.

Desire’s ember, glowing bright,
In fields where crimson steals the sight.
Lovers sigh in sweet delight,
Captured in the rapture’s light.

Vermilion hues in twilight's gleam,
Reflections of a vivid dream.
Passions sparked in evening air,
Awaken hearts beyond compare.

A breath, a touch, a burning glance,
In crimson's thrall, we’re lost, entranced.
Forgotten woes in scarlet kiss,
A world of nothing but pure bliss.

Crimson rapture, seize the day,
In vibrant love, we find our way.
For in the depths of ruby glow,
Eternal flames of passion flow.

Passion's Pirouette

In the silent depths of night, passion pirouettes
Two souls alight, their hearts a duet
With every twirl, their dreams unfold
In stories of love, timeless and bold

The moonlight casts a gentle glow
On faces flushed, lit from below
Each movement speaks of fervent grace
In their dance, they find their place

Emotions whirl in a fiery spree
A tempest of love, wild and free
In that fervent cadence, they forget
All but their passion's pirouette

Symphonic Affection

In melodies woven of love, soft and grand
Each note a whisper, as they understand
A symphony crafted by destiny's hand
Two hearts united, in harmonic strand

The violins hum, a tender embrace
Their souls entwined in a warm, loving space
With each crescendo, their spirits rise
To the heavens, where true love lies

Their affection sings, in chords so divine
A composition perfect, over time
In the grand opus of life, they reflect
Eternal love, in symphonic affect

Glistening Steps

Under starlit skies, their steps glisten bright
In the cool embrace of a moonlit night
Each footprint a promise, tenderly placed
Through the sands of time, their love is traced

With every step, their journey expands
In silent whispers, they understand
The path they tread, with courage and grace
Etched in the light of each other's face

In twilight's glow, their future unfurls
A tapestry woven with radiant pearls
Together they walk, in destiny's reps
Hand in hand, through glistening steps

Whispered Waltz

In the quietude of dusk, where shadows dance
Two lovers meet, by fate's own chance
In a waltz whispered, serene and slow
Their hearts synchronize, in gentle flow

Each movement a secret, only they know
In the cadence of love’s tender show
With eyes that speak, volumes untold
In the twilight, their romance bold

As the night blankets, with stars so bright
They whirl and twirl, consumed by light
In the silence of the whispered waltz
Their love finds voice, without a fault

Entwined in Elegance

In the dance of shadows, love alights,
Whispered secrets through the night.
Swaying softly, hearts combine,
Entwined in elegance, divine.

Moonlight smiles upon the scene,
Graceful steps, a lover's dream.
In the stillness, moments find,
A bond that's pure, souls entwined.

Beneath the stars, a silent pledge,
On the edge of time, love's ledge.
Fingers trace an artful sign,
Entwined in elegance, a rhyme.

Eternal waltz of night and day,
In this dance, we softly sway.
Hands together, yours and mine,
Entwined in elegance, we shine.

Cha-Cha of Attraction

Feet in motion, hearts align,
In the cha-cha, feelings shine.
A step to left, a skip to right,
Rhythm strikes, we're in the light.

Eyes lock in, a daring glance,
In this dance, we take a chance.
Passion's beat, a sweet seduction,
Cha-cha of attraction, no reduction.

Hands embrace, we spin around,
Lost in music, love profound.
Underneath the disco lights,
Cha-cha brings our hearts to heights.

Melody that pulls us near,
Every twirl, the night we cheer.
In the rhythm, pure connection,
Cha-cha of attraction, no reflection.

Enchanted Movements

Through the forest, whispers call,
Enchanted movements, we enthrall.
Underneath the ancient trees,
Magic stirs with every breeze.

Footsteps trace a sacred tune,
Dance beneath the silver moon.
Mystic air, with stars aligned,
In its weave, our hearts are signed.

We drift within a dreamlike trance,
Our spirits touch in nature's dance.
Every swirl, an artful breath,
Life ignited, beyond death.

In the glade, where light is spun,
Two become, and dance as one.
In this realm, our souls find sense,
Through enchanted movements, immense.

Symphony of Emotions

Notes of love in tender play,
Symphony of emotions sway.
Melodies of heart's delight,
In the dusk till morning light.

Chords that strum the inner soul,
Compose a verse that makes us whole.
Harmony in passion's wake,
A symphony for love's own sake.

In the concert of our dreams,
Each emotion, brightly beams.
Violins that cry in time,
Echoes of affection chime.

Soft refrain of whispered sighs,
In this music, we arise.
Together, in our own devotion,
A symphony of endless emotion.

Beats of Belonging

In every heart, a drum's soft beat,
Where dreams and sorrows often meet,
A rhythm shared by all who dare,
To find their place and be aware.

Hands that reach and hold so tight,
In the dark and in the light,
Fingers weave a bond so strong,
Collective tunes, a timeless song.

Whispers carried on the breeze,
Echoes call from distant seas,
Together, harmonies align,
A symphony both yours and mine.

Footsteps tracing paths of old,
Stories of the young and bold,
A dance of joy, a dance of pain,
In every heart, a sweet refrain.

In this circle, we belong,
United in our silent song,
To the beat we each contribute,
Voices rise, resonate, salute.

Emotional Cha-Cha

Across the floor, emotions sway,
A dance of night, a dance of day,
Hearts in sync, a rhythmic glide,
Two steps closer, side by side.

The tango of a stolen glance,
Passion’s dance, a wild romance,
Spins and twirls beneath the stars,
Silent whispers, hidden scars.

In every step, stories told,
Love anew and love grown old,
The cha-cha of a tearful smile,
Worth the risk, every mile.

Eyes that lock in knowing gaze,
Heat that burns in countless ways,
Hands that clasp, never tire,
Fueling hope, wild desire.

In this dance, we find our truth,
Moments brief, years of youth,
Gliding through life’s great ballet,
Feelings lead, feet obey.

Subtle Twirl

In the hush of dawn's first light,
A gentle twirl, pure delight,
Whispers soft, secrets shared,
Moments fragile, yet so dared.

A glance, a nod, understanding eyes,
Beneath the vast and open skies,
A dance of grace, serene and true,
In every turn, a bond renews.

Steps so soft, barely seen,
In between the unsaid, serene,
Intimate, this waltz of fate,
Embraced by time, we levitate.

In shadowed dusk, twin shadows merge,
In syncopated patterns, they surge,
Every motion a silent plea,
Every sigh, a melody.

In the subtle twirl of night,
Love hidden, out of sight,
We spin in whispered harmony,
Bound by what is yet to see.

Everlasting Glide

Through the windswept plains of time,
Together, side by side we climb,
In every stride, hearts coincide,
On this everlasting glide.

Hands entwined, a sacred prayer,
A journey brave beyond compare,
Across the tides, we boldly ride,
Seamlessly, our worlds collide.

Horizons broad, our dreams unfold,
Stories of the brave retold,
With every step, a promise sworn,
Together we transcend the morn.

In endless motion, faith abides,
A love that never, ever hides,
Graceful as the waves at sea,
Bound eternally, you and me.

Onward, ever, through the skies,
Past the tears and beyond goodbyes,
Together in this dance of pride,
On life's magnificent, everlasting glide.

Divine Connection

In silent whispers, the spirit soars
Beyond the stars, through astral doors
A bridge of light, ethereal beams
Connecting souls, weaving dreams

Celestial chords, a sacred song
In unity, we all belong
Unseen threads, binding tight
In the infinite, eternal night

Eyes closed, a cosmic dance
Lost in love, an endless trance
Sacred words, softly spoken
In this realm, we're never broken

Boundless realms of joy and peace
From earthly chains, sweet release
Infinite journeys, hearts pure and free
Eternal closeness, you and me

Guided by the divine and wise
A whisper of truth through open skies
Hands outstretched, the touch of grace
In this profound, timeless embrace

Affectionate Waltz

In candle’s glow, our shadows twirl
The room around us starts to whirl
Hand in hand, we softly glide
In sync with love’s eternal tide

Eyes locked tight, hearts in beat
We move as one, feeling the heat
Each step a note in our sweet song
Together, right where we belong

Soft whispers melt into the night
Two hearts in love, in pure delight
A dance that speaks in silent ways
An everlasting, loving gaze

The world fades out, just you and me
In this moment, we are free
Lost in love’s enchanting trance
Entranced within our sacred dance

With every turn, our souls align
A waltz that transcends space and time
With each embrace, our spirits fuse
In love's gentle, tender ruse

Glistening Grooves

Beneath the moon's soft silver light
We dance till dawn arrests the night
Glistening grooves beneath our feet
In rhythm, where our worlds meet

Stars above, a cosmic crowd
Music plays, we laugh out loud
Echoes of joy, pure and bright
In this spellbinding, endless night

Barefoot, free, on sandy shores
Leaving behind closed doors
Together, in this dance we find
A unity of heart and mind

Light of dawn, new day's embrace
We find our home in this place
Every step, a story told
In glistening grooves, our love unfolds

The rhythm's beat in harmony
Guiding us through destiny
With every move, our spirits dance
In the glow of love's deep trance

Midnight Merengue

Underneath the velvet sky
Stars like diamonds, way up high
We dance in rhythm, hand in hand
In this enchanted, moonlit land

Midnight winds weave through our hair
A merengue beats, we're without a care
Steps in sync, the night unfolds
In whispered tales and secrets told

The music plays, a siren's call
In its embrace, we find it all
A world that's spun in silver light
Lost in this dance, till morning light

Twirl and spin in joyful grace
In each other's arms, a warm embrace
Rhythms merge, our souls collide
In this duet, side by side

Moonlight fades, dawn breaks the spell
In our hearts, the memories dwell
Midnight merengue, soft and slow
In its magic, love will grow

Euphoria's Movement

In the dawn of moments rare,
Joy uplifts with gentle care.
Eyes of wonder, hearts declare,
Hopes aloft in morning air.

Dancing through the endless skies,
Dreams unwrap where passion lies.
Graceful arcs, we realize,
Euphoria, a sweet surprise.

Leaping past the tired days,
Love enshrined in bright displays.
Clouds depart to sunlit ways,
Euphoria, it always stays.

Rhythms hum in fervent tune,
Springtime blooms, a vast lagoon.
Life adorned in gold doubloon,
Euphoria, beneath the moon.

Moments whisper, gently sway,
Time transcends, as shadows play.
In our hearts, it finds its way,
Euphoria will never stray.

Sweethearts' Waltz

Underneath the evening's glow,
Whispers soft, the night does flow.
Hand in hand, as breezes blow,
Sweethearts' waltz, in love they show.

Eyes that meet, across the floor,
Hearts entwined forevermore.
Spinning light, through love's great door,
Sweethearts' waltz, forever soar.

Glimmering beneath the stars,
Soulmates twirl, without the scars.
Boundless love, free of the bars,
Sweethearts' waltz, to Venus, Mars.

In the silence, melodies,
Carry whispers on the breeze.
Love's embrace in minor keys,
Sweethearts' waltz, it brings such ease.

From the dusk till break of day,
Twirling in a love array.
Heartbeats hum in sweet display,
Sweethearts' waltz, will always stay.

Gleaming Pirouette

Shimmering in light's embrace,
Spirals dance with stunning grace.
Moonlit whispers find their place,
Gleaming pirouette in space.

Under stars, they twist and turn,
Hearts ablaze, with passion burn.
Midnight secrets to discern,
Gleaming pirouette, we yearn.

Waves of light, in silent streams,
Echo softly through our dreams.
Hopeful murmurs, golden beams,
Gleaming pirouette redeems.

Through the night and into dawn,
Graceful figures softly drawn.
Dancing till the break of morn,
Gleaming pirouette, reborn.

Bound by time yet free as air,
Movements speak beyond compare.
In the dance of life's affair,
Gleaming pirouette declare.

Subtle Sway

In the hush of twilight's call,
Softly swaying, trees stand tall.
Gentle whispers start to fall,
Subtle sway, they heed the thrall.

Breezes brush the meadow's bloom,
Nature's dance in twilight's room.
As the night begins to loom,
Subtle sway, in fragrant plume.

Through the fields, in moonlight's grace,
Shadows shift in soft embrace.
Heartbeats find a steady pace,
Subtle sway, in lovers' lace.

Stars alight in silent gleam,
Weaving through the night's soft dream.
In the world of starlit seam,
Subtle sway, a flowing stream.

Time dissolves in gentle hue,
Moments blend in shades of blue.
Life and love in rhythm true,
Subtle sway, through me and you.

Savor the Samba

In rhythms wild where hearts reside,
We twirl and dip, in fervent tide.
With every beat, emotions pour,
As feet imbue the earthen floor.

Bright skirts flare in a vivid bloom,
Echoes of joy in a crowded room.
Hands clasp tight, yet spirits soar,
Samba's fire ignites the core.

Under moon's gleam, shadows prance,
Lost in the fevered, sensuous dance.
Eyes that speak without a word,
In each twirl, our souls are heard.

Joy constrained in fluid grace,
Mirrored passion upon the face.
Enthralled by rhythm's boundless sea,
In samba's hold, we find we're free.

Heartfelt Foxtrot

In elegant lines, we sweep and sway,
Each step measured, come what may.
With poised hearts, this dance we court,
Grace and love in seamless fort.

Soft whispers melt in twilight's hue,
As glides unfold in shadows new.
Every turn a silent vow,
Binding hearts in rhythmic bow.

Timeless tale on a ballroom floor,
Foxtrot weaves forevermore.
Eyes unite in tender trance,
In syncopation, souls advance.

Gentle lead and soft pursuit,
In every dip, emotions root.
Held so close, yet worlds apart,
In foxtrot's beat, we bare our heart.

Velvet Movements

Velvet nights with stars concealed,
In movements slow, dreams revealed.
Subtle grace in midnight's fold,
Elegant tales in silence told.

Steps as soft as whispered wind,
In arms we find where we begin.
Timeless rhythm, sweet affair,
In velvet dance, we live with care.

Shadowed forms in lamplight gleam,
In every sway, we glimpse a dream.
Hearts align in softest beats,
In velvet touch, our love completes.

Time stands still in every glide,
In this waltz, our worlds collide.
Silent stories softly spun,
In velvet's hold, we dance as one.

Whispered Waltz

Whispers float on breezes soft,
In waltz we rise, both low and loft.
Gentle turns with hearts entwined,
In every beat, a love designed.

Moonlight paints our ballroom bright,
In each twirl, we chase the night.
Held so close, yet drifting far,
In whispered waltz, we find our star.

Barefoot dreams on polished floor,
Echoes linger, timeless lore.
With each pivot, worlds unfold,
In waltz's grasp, our tale retold.

Soft embrace, the music's voice,
In its lilt, we make our choice.
Guided by the moon's soft light,
In whispered waltz, we take flight.

Echoes of Affection

In the quiet, whispers blend,
Softly through the night they send,
Echoes of affection's might,
Dancing in the pale moonlight.

Hearts that beat in perfect time,
Woven in a tender rhyme,
Sweet connections, boundless grace,
Found within a warm embrace.

Fingers brush, a fleeting touch,
Promises that mean so much,
Every breath, a silent vow,
Felt as then, and feeling now.

Eyes that meet and never part,
Windows to a caring heart,
Silent words that love bestows,
In the gentle night's repose.

Time may pass, and time may pause,
Love endures without a cause,
Echoes linger, ever near,
In each heartbeat's soft revere.

Nightfall Foxtrot

Shadows stretch as daylight fades,
Moonlight casts its silver shades,
Whispers in the twilight air,
Nightfall foxtrot everywhere.

Stars aligned in cosmic dance,
Twirl and spin in life's romance,
Velvet skies and northern lights,
Weaving dreams of wondrous sights.

Footsteps on this stage of night,
Hearts that sync and spirits light,
Move as one with planets' flow,
In the dark's enchanting glow.

Murmurs soft within the breeze,
Night's embrace with gentle ease,
Steps that follow endless tides,
Guided by the stars' divides.

Dawn will come, the dance will change,
But these steps won't feel so strange,
For in every night's parade,
Memory's foxtrot never fades.

Shimmy of Hearts

Twilight paints the skies in hues,
Love's sweet waltz in every muse,
Hearts that shimmy to the tune,
Beneath the soft, white-faced moon.

Eyes that sparkle, softly gleam,
Love like whispers in a dream,
Sway and spin in tender flow,
Dancing hearts, a gentle glow.

Laughter lilts in rhythmic strides,
Tales in every glance confide,
Steps that trace a pathway neat,
Rhythms of the hearts so sweet.

Moments held in fragile space,
Captured in a warm embrace,
Love's soft shimmy never ends,
Bound in time, where spirit bends.

Night will fade, but not the spark,
Left within where hearts embark,
Shimmy on, through dark and light,
Evermore, with love so bright.

Joyful Jive

Breezes play a melody,
Dancing leaves in harmony,
Nature's joyful jive, divine,
Steps that beautifully align.

Sunsets paint the skies with cheer,
Whispered tunes for all to hear,
Feet that tap in unison,
Hearts that leap, embrace the sun.

Twinkling stars up in the skies,
Echo joy with silent sighs,
Every beat, a pulse of glee,
In this grand, celestial spree.

Hands that clasp, together sway,
Joyful jive, the night's ballet,
Spirits lift and boldly strive,
In the dance that keeps alive.

Laughter rings through moonlit trails,
Joyful hearts leave merry tales,
Life, a jive that's ever true,
Dances on for me and you.

Sentimental Steps

In twilight's gentle, golden hue,
We traced the path where roses grew,
Underneath the whispering trees,
We moved as one with graceful ease.

Each step a memory we revive,
With every heartbeat, more alive,
In these steps, our tale unfolds,
A dance of love that never grows old.

The stars above, our silent guide,
Reflections in your eyes, so wide,
Our shadows played on moonlit grass,
A waltz that time could not surpass.

In rhythm with the night's sweet song,
In each other's arms, we belong,
Through trials and time, and life's retreats,
Our hearts in tandem, love repeats.

Now as the dawn begins to shine,
Hand in hand, your heart in mine,
Sentimental steps we will retrace,
Forever bound in love's embrace.

Fleeting Fox Trot

Quick as the wind, we take the floor,
The music calls, we both implore,
In swift glissades, we find our pace,
A fleeting flash of pure embrace.

Our movements blend, a swift duet,
In every turn, there's no regret,
Through hall and heart, our spirits sync,
In every beat, our souls distinct.

The rhythm rises, feet in flight,
Swift and sure, as day meets night,
Energetic, wild, and yet so sweet,
Our hearts converge where rhythms meet.

With fleeting steps, we paint the air,
A dance so free, beyond compare,
In moments brief, yet passion strong,
We find our place where we belong.

When music fades and silence grows,
The memory of our dance still flows,
A fleeting fox trot, fast yet pure,
In love's quick steps, forever secure.

Dancing Embrace

In the dance of dusk and dawn,
Where shadows bid the light so long,
Our hands find each other's clasp,
In an embrace where hearts relasp.

In the hush of evening glow,
Where whispers of the breezes blow,
We move in tandem, soul and grace,
Forever bound in this embrace.

Each twirl and dip, a soft caress,
In motion, we find our bliss,
The world fades behind our eyes,
In this dance, no more disguise.

Against the canvas of the night,
Our silhouettes in soft moonlight,
Hold tight this moment, pure and true,
Dancing embrace, just me and you.

As morning steals the night away,
Our dance may end but hearts will stay,
Forever held in love's sweet trace,
The memory of our dancing embrace.

Cupid's Quickstep

In the rush of love’s pursuit,
Our footsteps fall, resolute,
Cupid’s arrow, sharp and swift,
Guides our feet with gentle lift.

Quick step echoes in the hall,
As hearts align, we heed the call,
Through every twist and every turn,
In passion’s fire, our spirits burn.

We dance beneath the starry sky,
Where whispering winds of love fly,
In every glance and every smile,
Love’s quick step makes the night worthwhile.

With each movement, hearts ignite,
In the rhythm of the night,
Cupid’s game in love’s grand hall,
Holds us in its sweet enthrall.

When morning comes with soft sunrise,
We greet the day with opened eyes,
In love’s quickstep, swift and pure,
Together always, love’s allure.

Whirling Hearts

In a meadow softly graced,
Two hearts start to intertwine.
Moonlight whispers, love embraced,
In a dance that knows no time.

Petals swirl beneath their feet,
Softly carried on the breeze.
Twilight hours, moments sweet,
Hearts are whirling, feeling free.

Stars alight their secret vow,
Eyes locked in a silent dream.
Whirling hearts, in rhythm now,
Flowing like a gentle stream.

Bound by love's enchanting spell,
In this dance they find their peace.
Every step, a tale to tell,
Endless love will never cease.

Moonlit Waltz

Underneath the pale moon's glow,
Shadows waltz with tender grace.
In the night, love's whispers grow,
Two souls lost in sweet embrace.

Stars above, their silent throng,
Witness to the lovers' sway.
Moonlit waltz, a timeless song,
Hearts align and find their way.

Glistening paths of silver light,
Chart their course across the sky.
In this dance, the world feels right,
Truth revealed in every sigh.

Boundless night, a sacred stage,
For the waltz that ne'er will part.
Step by step, they turn the page,
Writing love with every heart.

Sway of Love

In a garden lush and wide,
Two hearts move in perfect time.
In their dance, no need to hide,
Love expressed in every rhyme.

Softly swaying to a tune,
Secret melodies they share.
Underneath the gentle moon,
Eyes that sparkle, souls laid bare.

Every step a sweet caress,
In the sway of love they find,
Moments filled with tenderness,
Weaving threads of hearts entwined.

Rain of petals from above,
Echoes of their whispered vow.
In the rhythm of their love,
Every heartbeat, here and now.

Eternal Tango

On a stage of endless night,
Two hearts play their timeless part.
In a dance of pure delight,
Eternal tango, work of art.

Glances stolen, passions flare,
Bodies close, their breath as one.
In the moon's soft, tender glare,
Tango's tale has just begun.

Movements fuse and tensions rise,
Hearts entwined in fierce embrace.
In their eyes, the fire lies,
Etched in every fleeting trace.

Bound forever in this dance,
Soul to soul, they hear the call.
Life and love, a grand romance,
Tango's steps, they heed them all.

Ballroom Fantasy

In gowns adorned with silver light,
Partners dance, hearts take their flight,
Beneath the chandelier's glow,
In a waltz, emotions flow.

Twirl in rhythm, steps align,
Whispers blend with violin,
Masks conceal but eyes reveal,
Mysteries that dreams unseal.

Crimson roses, fragrant breath,
Moments dance from life to death,
Echoes ring through polished floors,
As love in motion softly soars.

Moonlight through the windows streams,
Casting shadows, painting dreams,
Time dissolves in graceful sweep,
In this fantasy, souls keep.

When music fades to morning's hue,
Footprints fade, but love stays true,
In the ballroom of the heart,
We are never far apart.

Glide of Tenderness

Soft the breeze, the willow sways,
Whispers of the past embrace,
In footsteps light, we find our way,
Through fields of gold, lost in grace.

Hearts entwine with silent ease,
Love's soft murmur through the trees,
In every touch a gentle trace,
A world suspended, time's sweet freeze.

Eyes meet eyes, a story told,
In quiet moments we behold,
The dance of souls, serene and kind,
Where hearts in harmony unwind.

Each step a note in love's grand score,
Together we seek evermore,
Through softest hues of dawn and night,
In tenderness, the world ignites.

Promises in whispers made,
In glides so soft, our fears allayed,
With every breath, a vow renewed,
To love in tenderness subdued.

Jazz of the Heart

Saxophones with soulful cries,
Notes that rise to starry skies,
Rhythms pulse like heartbeat's call,
In jazzy nights, we lose it all.

Trumpets blaze with golden fire,
Pianos hum what hearts desire,
Basslines thread through midnight blue,
In smoky clubs, our hearts construe.

Improvise through life's refrain,
Laughter, love, and sweet refrain,
In melodies that twist and swing,
A jazz of hearts in union bring.

Sip the wine of fleeting nights,
In syncopated, joyful flights,
Dancers lost in groovy spell,
In music's thrall, our spirits dwell.

When dawn breaks through the smoky haze,
Memories like soft brass stays,
In notes that linger, echoes part,
In jazz we find the beat of heart.

Eternal Spirals

Stars in cosmic dance engage,
Galaxies on Heaven’s stage,
In spirals vast, through time we move,
The universe in endless groove.

Planets waltz in rhythmic spin,
Orbit traces from within,
Eternal paths of light and dark,
In void and matter, spirits arc.

Nebulae in colors blend,
From birth to death, life transcends,
In every spiral, stories weave,
Of dreams conceived and hearts to grieve.

Comets streak on journeys vast,
Through eons that forever last,
In cosmic spirals, futures trace,
The dance of time, life's gentle grace.

In the infinite expanse,
Eternal spirals lead the dance,
In ever-turning cosmic spree,
We find our place in destiny.

Blush of Dusk

In twilight's soft and silent rush,
The sky ignites in vivid blush,
Shadows stretch, as stars awake,
Whispers of night softly partake.

The horizon's edge, a canvas stark,
Where day and night yet make their mark,
Gold and purple gently blend,
As day to night begins to send.

Barely heard, the whispered breeze,
Through rustling leaves of solemn trees,
Crickets sing their twilight song,
In dusk's embrace, we all belong.

Golden Embrace

Sunlight spills in golden streams,
Kissing fields and whispering dreams,
Embers in the morning light,
Chasing shadows from the night.

Waves of warmth in soft cascade,
Nature's fabric brightly laid,
Petals stretch to morning's grace,
Touching souls with tender trace.

Meadows hum with gentle sighs,
In the dawn, we rise, surmise,
Beneath the tree's encircling brace,
We feel the golden day's embrace.

Silken Spin

Threads of silk on morning's breath,
Spinning tales of life and death,
Nature's loom in constant spin,
Weave the world where dreams begin.

Dewdrops cling to gossamer,
Diamonds in the dawn's whisper,
Spiders' artistry untold,
Beauty in the web's hold.

Softly weaving, shadows dance,
In the light of morning's trance,
Silken threads in gentle spin,
Craft the day from where we’ve been.

Heavenly Sway

Stars align in gentle sway,
Guiding night and marking day,
Mystic rhythms in the sky,
Silent whispers from on high.

The moonlight baths the world in sheen,
Silver hues in tranquil scene,
Constellations softly gleam,
In the heavens' silent theme.

Galaxies in spiral flight,
Paint the canvass of the night,
In the cosmos vast array,
Find the soul's heavenly sway.

Velvet Rhythm

Soft like velvet, whispers dance
Through the night, they take their chance
Stars align in rhythmic hue
Moonlight bathes the world anew

Hearts beat gently, synchro-tied
By the evening's gentle tide
Dreams arise in shadowed scenes
Velvet whispers, tender dreams

Forward, backward, step and turn
All around the starlights burn
Velvet rhythm, crescent tune
Holds the night in sweet cocoon

Hands entwined and fingers glide
Silent symphonies implied
Lovers swaying, dark and bright
Velvet rhythm, through the night

Fleeting Footsteps

Footsteps fleeting on the breeze
Whispers lost among the trees
Shadows dance, where dawn retreats
Softly, life the night completes

Silent echoes fade away
Marking time of night and day
Moonlit path and hidden dreams
Fleeting footsteps, twilight beams

Lives entwined on gossamer thread
Interwoven paths we've tread
Moments passing, like a sigh
Fleeting footsteps, nights gone by

Stars above in silent sweep
Guard the secrets we can't keep
Footprints lead, yet disappear
Fleeting steps, from far to near

Midnight Minuet

Moon ascending, night so still
Stars align with quiet thrill
Soft embrace of darkened air
Midnight dance, beyond compare

Whispers carry on the breeze
Secrets told among the trees
Footsteps weave a quiet spell
Midnight tales they softly tell

Echoes rise within the night
Waltzing shadows, soft and light
Midnight minuet begins
Music flows where time has thinned

Hearts in rhythm, souls align
Lost in midnight's tender sign
Every step a whispered note
Midnight minuet, we float

Dreamlike Duet

Silent whispers in the night
Dreams that take their gentle flight
Starry skies and moonlit dreams
Dreamlike duet, flowing streams

Echoes blend in harmony
Two souls dance in unity
Melodies of night unite
Dreams sustain the silent flight

Hands entwined in twilight air
Symphony beyond compare
Moonlight leads the lovers' tune
Dreamlike duet, whispered swoon

Hearts as one, the night their stage
Eternity upon each page
Dreams and whispers intertwine
Dreamlike duet, pure divine

Choreographed Love

In rhythm's dance, our hearts do sway,
With tender glances, night and day.
Steps align in perfect time,
Choreographed, our love's sublime.

A gentle spin, your hand in mine,
In mirrored moves, our souls combine.
Whispers soft in twilight's glow,
Together, to the stars, we flow.

With every beat, our bond grows strong,
In unison, where we belong.
Bound by fate, our feet embrace,
A timeless waltz through time and space.

A dip, a twirl, we lose control,
In this eternal, graceful role.
Love's ballet, a sight to see,
Two hearts dancing, wild and free.

As music fades, we're still enshrined,
In love's performance, so entwined.
Our love, a dance that's ever true,
Choreographed by me and you.

Twisting Embrace

Beneath the stars, our bodies curl,
In twists of love, our hearts unfurl.
A touch, a sigh, we intertwine,
In this embrace, forever mine.

A tangled mass of limbs so tight,
We find our haven in the night.
With every twist, our spirits soar,
In love's embrace, we seek for more.

A tender grip, a loving gaze,
With every turn, we set ablaze.
Bound by passion's fierce delight,
We twist in love through darkest night.

Our bodies move, a seamless weave,
Together, in each other's sleeve.
A dance of love, so wild and pure,
In twisting embrace, we find our cure.

With every breath, our flames ignite,
In twisting love, we find our light.
Together, hearts both young and free,
In this embrace, eternally.

Harmony of Affection

In love's sweet notes, we find our song,
A melody where we belong.
Each chord, a promise, pure and true,
In harmony, just me and you.

A symphony of tender care,
In every note, our hearts laid bare.
The harmony that binds us tight,
In love's embrace, forever right.

With each caress, our theme unfolds,
In gentle tones, our story told.
A duet of affection's grace,
In harmony, our perfect place.

A gentle hum, a loving tune,
Our hearts aligned beneath the moon.
In every beat, our love expressed,
In harmony, we find our rest.

Together, we compose our fate,
With every note, we resonate.
A harmony of love's affection,
A timeless bond, our true connection.

Moonlit Waltz

Under the moon's soft, silver gleam,
We waltz beneath the night's serene.
With every step, our spirits rise,
In moonlit waltz, we touch the skies.

A gentle spin, your hand in mine,
While stars above in silence shine.
Our hearts in sync, with every sway,
In moonlit dance, we find our way.

The night embraces us so tight,
In moonlit waltz, we're lost in light.
With every turn, our love grows deep,
In moon's soft glow, our secrets keep.

Each movement whispers love so true,
In moonlit magic, me and you.
A dance that binds our souls as one,
Beneath the stars and moonlit sun.

As moonlight fades, the night is gone,
Our love's waltz carries on.
In dreams we dance, in moon's embrace,
A timeless waltz through endless space.

Zephyr's Dance

In twilight's gentle, soft embrace,
Where shadows twirl, begin their chase,
The zephyr whispers through the trees,
A secret carried by the breeze.

Leaves flutter like a lover's sigh,
Kissed by the winds that pass them by,
A pirouette in evening's glow,
A dance the world will never know.

Stars peek through the velvet sky,
As nightfall's curtain rises high,
Their light, a partner to the air,
In rhythms only nature shares.

Through meadows where the flowers bloom,
And spread their petals, sweet perfume,
The zephyr twines with every grace,
A ballet time cannot erase.

In stillness, let your spirit soar,
And feel the wind forevermore,
For in its dance, you'll surely find,
A moment's peace for heart and mind.

Midnight Masquerade

Beneath the glow of silver moon,
Shadows waltz to night's sweet tune,
Masked in mystery, darkened guise,
A ball of stars within our eyes.

Oceans whisper to the shore,
Secrets kept forevermore,
In the dance of dark and light,
Mysteries of the endless night.

Trees cast silhouettes on ground,
Silent watchers all around,
Their branches swaying, shadows play,
In silver light, till break of day.

The night is vaster than it seems,
A world alive in endless dreams,
With every star that graces sky,
A tale where fantasies can fly.

In quietness, hearts find their speed,
In moonlit paths we all may heed,
The masquerade, forever grand,
Where night takes time by the hand.

Whispered Melody

In fields where golden grasses sway,
A whispered song begins to play,
The tune, a secret soft and low,
In nature's breath it starts to grow.

Through rustling leaves and babbling streams,
It floats within our quiet dreams,
A lullaby of earth and sky,
That carries souls where eagles fly.

In tender notes the song is spun,
By moon and stars till night is done,
A harmony of life and lore,
In whispered verses to explore.

Each note a call, each word a kiss,
A melody that's born from bliss,
It weaves a path through time and space,
An echo of the heart's embrace.

So listen close, let silence speak,
In every quiet, moments seek,
The whispered melody that's free,
A timeless song of unity.

Dewdrops' Waltz

Upon the petals morning kissed,
Where dewdrops rest in gentle mist,
A waltz begins as sunlight shows,
And in its dance, a garden grows.

Each droplet sparkles with the dawn,
Reflecting hues as night is gone,
In graceful steps they slide and glide,
Nature’s jewels in morning's pride.

Beneath the sky's soft azure lace,
The dewdrops find their perfect place,
They twirl and spin in soft caress,
A ballet of pure tenderness.

Their fleeting dance, a beauty rare,
An ode to life in morning air,
Ephemeral yet full of grace,
A symphony in nature's space.

So cherish dawn’s first gentle gleam,
Where dewdrops dance and moments dream,
For in the waltz of morning’s light,
We find new hope and endless sight.

Lover's Sashay

Beneath the moon's soft gentle sway,
Two hearts entwined, they gently lay.
With every step, a silent grace,
In each embrace, they find their place.

Their shadows waltz upon the shore,
A dance of love forevermore.
With whispered vows and tender glance,
They lose themselves within the dance.

Stars reflect in lover's eyes,
A symphony beneath the skies.
In cadence pure, they drift away,
In lover's arms, they'll always stay.

Time does slow within this trance,
As every heartbeat fuels the dance.
In rhythm true, they hold their way,
Their souls refreshed by lover's sashay.

As dawn awakens night's repose,
Their love, like tides, forever flows.
In every spin and every glide,
In love, they live, and there abide.

Timeless Twirl

Within the clock's eternal spin,
Two souls unite, the dance begin.
Each second ticks, a step anew,
In harmony, their spirits flew.

Beneath the skies that time has kissed,
Their love entwined in endless twist.
With every turn, the world stands still,
In timeless twirl, they feel the thrill.

The music plays, an ageless tune,
They dance beneath the ageless moon.
In rhythm pure, they chase the stars,
Their hearts as one, no time's cruel bars.

Each heartbeat echoes through the night,
Two souls in dance, a wondrous sight.
In step and twirl, they find their way,
In timeless love, both night and day.

As ages pass and years unfold,
Their love remains, a tale retold.
In every twirl, their hearts exclaim,
In timeless dance, they stay the same.

Devoted Duet

Two voices blend in perfect song,
A melody where hearts belong.
With every note, their love expressed,
In devoted duet, they're truly blessed.

Harmony binds their souls as one,
A symphony begun and done.
In every chord, a vow they weave,
In each refrain, their spirits cleave.

Their voices rise, a tender plea,
In unison, they find the key.
Their hearts align in pure duet,
In love's embrace, they never fret.

Notes cascade like gentle rain,
In unity, they share no pain.
With every verse, their love is set,
In devoted song, they never forget.

As echoes fade into the night,
Their love remains, a constant light.
In every tune and every beat,
Their devoted duet is ever sweet.

Harmony in Motion

In graceful sway, two lovers go,
In harmony, their spirits flow.
With every step, their hearts align,
In motion pure, a love divine.

Their feet caress the earth so light,
In dance, they chase the endless night.
With every spin, their souls uplift,
In motion's grace, their love's sweet gift.

The world becomes a fleeting blur,
In harmony, their spirits stir.
With each embrace, the moment stills,
In unified hearts, their love fulfills.

Beneath the stars, they find their way,
In motion's dance, their hearts convey.
In rhythm true, they form a spell,
In harmony, all fears they quell.

Through life's grand waltz, they glide so free,
In dance, they find their destiny.
In every twirl, a dream in motion,
In harmony, they share devotion.

Aurora's Caress

A sky of fire and tender grace,
Aurora's lights, a grand embrace.
The stars give way to dawning hue,
A morning kissed with shades of blue.

Her fingers brush the night away,
With every beam, a brand-new day.
Mountains blush with a gentle glow,
As rivers sparkle down below.

In silence deep, the world awaits,
While nature paints with softest traits.
Birdsong echoes, breaking dawn,
A lullaby until the morn.

Mist rises from the cooling earth,
Whispers of a daily birth.
Aurora’s kiss, a fleeting spell,
Bids the night a soft farewell.

On fields of gold, the shadows fade,
Life renews in every glade.
Her touch, a promise, pure and true,
A world reborn, each day anew.

Gossamer Glide

In twilight's soft and subtle sheen,
A gossamer of dreams unseen.
Fairies dance on zephyrs light,
Spinning whispers in the night.

Each thread of mist, a silken touch,
Where moonbeams shimmer, cannot clutch.
Stars above, a silvery guide,
With every step, the world grows wide.

Petals bathe in lunar glow,
Where secrets of the midnight flow.
A ballet of the fleeting dreams,
Through silent woods and starlit streams.

Beneath the canopy of time,
A phantom waltz, a silent chime.
Soft as shadows, light as breath,
They drift between the life and death.

In velvet night, their whispers fade,
A fleeting dance in quiet glade.
Come dawn, their presence slips away,
But in the heart, their dreams will stay.

Enchanted Steps

In glades where sunlight gently spills,
Enchanted steps mark ancient thrills.
The forest breathes a secret song,
Where whispered tales and shadows throng.

Amid the dance of leaves and light,
A chime of joy, a burst of sprite.
Each step ignites a magic trace,
In this secluded, sacred place.

Beneath the boughs of emerald green,
A world unseen, a tranquil scene.
Creatures small with eyes aglow,
Join the dance in evening's flow.

Barefoot prints on mossy ground,
Where faeries tread without a sound.
Every leap and twirl, a spell,
In sylvan realms where wonders dwell.

As dusk descends and shadows play,
The dance persists till break of day.
Enchanted steps, a fleeting glance,
Of nature's hidden, wild romance.

Heartbeat Ballet

Within the soul, a rhythm beats,
A ballet where the heart retreats.
Emotions twirl in silent grace,
On love's soft stage, they find their place.

With every pulse, a story told,
Of dreams embraced and secrets bold.
In choreographed serenity,
They dance the steps of destiny.

A leap of faith, a pirouette,
Where hope and sorrow gently met.
In cadence with the breath of time,
They weave a mystical, sweet rhyme.

In tender waltz, the heart reveals,
Each scar it bears, each pain it heals.
A symphony of joys and fears,
Composed of laughter, woven with tears.

The curtain falls, yet still the beat,
Continues in its dance so sweet.
This heartbeat ballet, love's decree,
An endless, timeless reverie.

Ephemeral Groove

Beneath the moon's soft glow,
We dance where shadows play,
In the night's ebb and flow,
Dreams flicker, then fade away.

Music whispers through the air,
Our feet trace fleeting trails,
Moments brief yet rare,
In twilight's gentle veils.

Stars above begin to weep,
For time that slips unseen,
In this groove, a secret we keep,
A bond, though ever lean.

Hands interlace, then part,
As dawn begins to stir,
Yet forever in our hearts,
Lingers that night, a blur.

Ephemeral as the breeze,
That stirs the morning dew,
In memories' gentle tease,
We find that groove anew.

Hearts in Motion

Kisses soft like moonlit rain,
Hearts in motion, pure and free,
Through joy and tender pain,
We dance in endless sea.

Eyes that speak in silent words,
Gazes met, an ardent flame,
Love's song like chirping birds,
An eternal, sweet refrain.

Steps in perfect harmony,
Hands entwined in promised vow,
Bound by love's deep alchemy,
Together, here and now.

In the rush of life's embrace,
Moments still, then swiftly gone,
Yet in every gentle trace,
We find where we belong.

Hearts in motion, boundless, true,
Through life’s ever-shifting tides,
Together, me and you,
Our love forever guides.

Waltz of Love

Soft as dawn's first light,
We begin our waltz of love,
Guided by stars so bright,
Blessed by heavens above.

Steps that glide serene,
Hearts that beat as one,
In a graceful, tender scene,
Our journey just begun.

Eyes that tell a tale,
Beyond the spoken word,
In love, we shall prevail,
Together, unperturbed.

Moonlit nights and sunlit days,
In each other's arms we twirl,
Lost in love’s sweet haze,
Our dance becomes a pearl.

Waltz with me forever,
Through time’s unending dance,
Bound by love, we never,
Shall miss another chance.

Tango of Souls

In shadows deep, where secrets bloom,
We dance, the tango of souls,
Passion ignites the room,
In love's immersive roles.

Eyes that pierce the night,
Desire in every glance,
In motion's flowing flight,
Our spirits find their trance.

Steps weave a tale of fire,
Hearts entwine with fervent beat,
In this fervent gyre,
Life’s melody, bittersweet.

Under stars' watchful gaze,
Silent words are spoken,
Lost in passion's maze,
No bounds can be broken.

Tango, fierce and pure,
In each other’s arms, we find,
The souls' dance we endure,
Eternally intertwined.

Enraptured Steps

In twilight's gentle glow, we meet
Two shadows merging, soft and fleet
With each step, a story spun
Enraptured hearts, two beats as one

Beneath the moon's envious gaze
Our dance a whisper, tender haze
Every movement, brush of air
Enchanted realm, beyond compare

Silence speaks in hushed caress
In perfect unison, we bless
Night's embrace, a fragile thread
Upon this path, by passion led

No words can capture what we weave
In fleeting moments, never leave
Steps that echo, timeless dance
In love's deep trance, a bold romance

Endless waltz beneath the stars
Our spirits bound, no prison bars
With each twirl, a promise kept
In dreams, forever we have stept

Elegant Pirouette

Whispers of wind in her flowing dress
Each twirl, a symphony of finesse
Her heart aligns with every spin
In each pirouette, a world within

The stage alight with a gentle grace
In shadows, light finds its place
Each turn, a delicate ballet
In movement, night turns to day

Elegance paints arcs in the sky
With each leap, she seems to fly
A ballerina's soft refrain
In dance, her burdens wane

The music calls, she heeds its plea
Her form a whisper, wild and free
In pirouette, the world stands still
Elegance, she holds the quill

A final bow, a soft adieu
With grace, she moves into the blue
Her dance, a story etched in light
Pirouettes, eternal flight

Heartbeat Mambo

In the pulse of a vibrant beat
Our bodies sway, our spirits meet
Heartbeat mambo, wild and free
Lost in rhythm, you and me

Feet that move in syncopation
Heartbeats match with verification
Every step a bold embrace
In this dance, we find our place

Twisting, turning, pulse entwined
In the music, all aligned
The rhythm takes us, no retreat
Together in this heartbeat beat

Eyes that shimmer, breath that melds
In each other’s arms, we're held
Heartbeat mambo, pure delight
In this dance, we own the night

As the final note descends
Our enchanted evening ends
Yet the rhythm in our veins
In heartbeat mambo, love remains

Graceful Tango

Under amber lights, we meet
Two dancers in the twilight heat
With every step, a story told
Graceful tango, fierce yet bold

In each movement, hearts do speak
A tethered spell, both strong and weak
Eyes that lock, a daring glance
In tango's rhythm, we entrace

The floor a canvas, we two paint
In every turn, a sweet constraint
Tempered passion, masterful flair
In tandem steps, beyond compare

A whispered sigh, a gentle clasp
In tango’s grip, a fervent grasp
Every pivot, soul's expose
In dance, emotions elegantly play

As music fades, the night succumbs
In memories, our tango hums
A dance of grace, an artful show
In graceful tango, love does grow

Sweep of Sentiments

In the hush of twilight, dreams take flight,
Through corridors of memory, they weave.
Whispered echoes of the night,
In every heartbeat, they believe.

Shadows dance with moonlight's grace,
Time’s embrace, both kind and cruel.
In the mirror of a lover's face,
Visions bloom both fierce and fragile.

Sweeping through the halls of thought,
Feelings rise like morning mist.
Unspoken words, emotions caught,
In the gentle twilight, kissed.

Journey through the night’s soft veil,
Hearts alight in sterling bright.
In the silence, voices sail,
Through the corridors of night.

Sweep of sentiments so deep,
Cradle dreams in quiet keep.
In hearts where shadows gently creep,
Waking worlds from slumbered sleep.

Twinkling Tides

Beneath the sky's adorned expanse,
Stars alight in cosmic dance.
Waves alight in moon's embrace,
Sea and sky in twinkling trance.

Whispers of the ocean's song,
Echoed where the stars belong.
Tides that carry dreams along,
In the night, a tranquil throng.

Moonbeams paint the water's crest,
With silver gleams, the ocean's vest.
In dreams, the soul finds rest,
Upon the shore, a heartfelt quest.

Every wave a tale unfolds,
Of treasures hidden, secrets told.
Mysteries in rhythms rolled,
By the stars and waters bold.

Twinkling tides of timeless grace,
Nature's beauty, time's embrace.
In the dance, we find our place,
In the night, a boundless space.

Unison Waltz

Amidst the twilight's gentle hue,
Dances intertwined as two.
Hearts that beat in perfect sync,
In the waltz, their spirits link.

Stars above that softly gleam,
Cast their glow upon the stream.
Two souls joined in life's sweet dream,
Dance as one, a seamless team.

Hand in hand, they turn and twirl,
In a world of moonlight swirl.
In each other, they unfurl,
Love's sweet dance, a precious pearl.

Steps that echo through the night,
Whispers soft in silver light.
In their eyes, the stars ignite,
In the waltz, they find delight.

Unison in every stride,
Hearts that never seek to hide.
In the dance, their love is wide,
In the waltz, both true and tied.

Undying Waltz

In the garden, shadows play,
Underneath the dying day.
Waltz of whispers, night and day,
Love that never shall decay.

Candles flicker in the breeze,
Memories like autumn leaves.
In the dance, the heart believes,
In each step, the soul retrieves.

Through the years, their passion flows,
In every step, love's ember glows.
In the waltz, the moment shows,
Eternal bond that never slows.

Hand in hand, they drift through time,
In a love that's so sublime.
In their hearts, the perfect rhyme,
In the waltz, forever prime.

Undying waltz, in twilight's kiss,
Sealed with every turn in bliss.
In the dance, they find their bliss,
In the waltz, the endless kiss.

Milton Keynes UK
Ingram Content Group UK Ltd.
UKHW042047210624
444555UK00014B/664